# Gateless Menagerie

# Gateless Menagerie

Larry D. Thacker

Gateless Menagerie
Copyright © 2021 Larry D. Thacker
All Rights Reserved.
Published by Unsolicited Press.
Printed in the United States of America.
First Edition 2021.

No part of this book may be used or reproduced in any manner whatsoever without written permission except in the case of brief quotations embodied in critical articles or reviews.

Portions of this book are works of fiction. Any references to historical events, real people, or real places are used fictitiously. Other names, characters, places and events are products of the author's imagination, and any resemblances to actual events or places or persons, living or dead, is entirely coincidental.

Attention schools and businesses: for discounted copies on large orders, please contact the publisher directly. Books are brought to the trade by Ingram.

For information contact:
Unsolicited Press
Portland, Oregon
www.unsolicitedpress.com
orders@unsolicitedpress.com
619-354-8005

Cover Design: Kathryn Gerhardt
Editor: Kay Grey

ISBN: 978-1-950730-79-7

# Contents

| | |
|---|---|
| This | 13 |
| Animal, thou shalt | 14 |
| Relief within Arm's Reach | 15 |
| Tale of the orange-throated whiptail lizard | 18 |
| The pair in the woods | 19 |
| The woods blindly fatten up | 20 |
| What did I want? | 21 |
| Where were they going? | 22 |
| Backward Spiritual | 24 |
| The Orange-Throated Whiptail Considers | 26 |
| Friday Night | 27 |
| The cat's paw prints in this morning's snow offers no sound | 28 |
| An Endurance III | 29 |
| Daily Rhapsody | 31 |
| Some days it's that delicious parade | 33 |
| Dead cat circled in turkeys | 35 |
| There are no mile markers in space. | 37 |
| The Gods of Firsts and Companions | 38 |
| Menagerie | 43 |

| | |
|---|---|
| I turn on the early morning news, | 44 |
| Mid-Day Film Editing | 45 |
| Re-Coil | 46 |
| Today is Saturday. Pick your headline. | 48 |
| I was warned in school against reading ahead: | 49 |
| Let Off To Run, Part I | 51 |
| Micro-Biology | 52 |
| I sip my Red Stripe beer, as usual, | 53 |
| The Changing | 54 |
| Along Middle-August, Summer Thinks | 55 |
| They Call Me | 56 |
| Familiarity | 57 |
| I Divine | 59 |
| Swamp at Cape Fear | 61 |
| A teaspoon of the star's collapsed core weighs a billion tons | 63 |
| Railroad Song | 64 |
| Murakami Steak & Eggs | 66 |
| The Rumor | 67 |
| Let Off To Run, Part II | 68 |
| We Learn from History | 69 |
| Night & Day | 70 |
| I've been grounding myself lately. | 71 |

| | |
|---|---|
| Yellow Found | 72 |
| I like waking up early | 73 |
| Youtube: The Hand of God | 74 |
| Creekside | 76 |
| Being | 77 |
| Reading a New Poem | 79 |
| The Morning's Crow Math | 80 |
| Birth Right | 81 |
| First Come, First Served | 82 |
| Interpretation | 84 |
| Between Worlds | 86 |
| Azure Cold | 87 |
| The Same Question, Again. | 88 |
| Bosch Studies on Monsters I, II, & III | 89 |
| Peck: A making of stars | 90 |
| The Baby Visits | 92 |
| These Things | 94 |
| What Slight Dissonance | 96 |
| Telling the Humans | 97 |
| Eroding to Sleep | 98 |
| Sunken Ground | 99 |
| Let's agree | 100 |

# Acknowledgements

Mid-Day Film Editing      *Sonic Boom*
Earliest      *Warren Anthology*
Yellow Found      *Everyday Poems*
Re-Coil      *Poetry South*
Creekside      *Yellow Chair Review*
These Things      *The Hungry Chimera*
Eroding to Sleep      *Boned Stories*

For my mother,
strolling in lands
on the other side
of the gate

# This

will be just about right for what you need,
for as long as you have attention for it.

It's winter now, but a sixty-degree memory
of spring wants us to never forget,
so all the seasonal gears necessary to render us
amazed and helpless are mustered up,
when only last week it was
                                    below zero for days.

And now cardinals play in the field
like streaks of red and brown questions,
new insects are born out, swarming into light
as if they have more than a few days at it.

The squirrels jostle old leaves as if snow
isn't called for by the weekend. But for whatever time
it all lasts,
        for however clueless we beings seem,

there's always someone nearby willing
to remind us softly:

                it is what it is.

# Animal, thou shalt

take down your prey by the kicking hindquarters,
the ragged and flailing tail, the muddy hooves,

sink and tear fangs through hunched and bucking
spiny backbone, stripping flesh, spraying blood,

clutch the quickened, tempting pulse of throats
in the finally exhausted young, the slowed pulse

of the infirm and aged, nip the heels and howl
the long songs of sweetly soaked readied meat,

run rivers red with news of your bright kingdom.

## Relief within Arm's Reach

A giggly laugh blankets
with its mumble of waiting,
sweaty with unsteady ink,

flapping over us
like a self-appointed angel,
out of breath with a rush of half-promises,

wing-halted on the inner-glass
of the inescapable room
of emergencies,

folding in on a slow creep,
three-in-the-morning-chaos
and a lethargy no one escapes,

scent of vomit
just under bleach and perfume
sweetens

unanswered grunts and groans,
names darted out
over the rocking vessel

of pain – cloud
of seated misery without oars,
set adrift each night,

thumbs working, cells chiming,
bouncing knees, nodding heads,
drooling homeless man leaning nearer

the girl applying fresh red
to lips, all
Murakami dream-swirl.

A blanket-swaddled tiny service dog yips
at the Elvis-looking custodian
rolling though with a clean-up kit,

double-door still refuses entry
no matter how long you stare
and wonder who's back there,

writhing, lurching,
stiffening, then,
finally, a form of sleeping.

There, a mask, covering what?
An illness brought in, or
something to avoid?

Some choke down the obligatory coffee
long-cooled and bittered, ghost
of what it should be,

it, too, wondering, when the sun comes.
At around four-thirty everyone inhales
that same prayer, familiar,

let us be gone from here
when we awake, let us be free
of this vessel of hell,

this next cursed breath.

# Tale of the orange-throated whiptail lizard

Is it an idea the creature has, this changing for the better?
Too early in the stage to call it evolution, the thing

only knows a millennial-long discomfort passed on
by stories, expressed now in its own life, a quirk

or such in its day ranging from bothersome to deadly
inconvenient. It can't go on like this, the animal realizes.

Can we assume it's like that? That down in the well of DNA,
something without ears listens, has been listening, forever,

and finally hears, shifts, sends words out over the millions
of miles of twisting backbone, one to the other to another,

at such infinitesimal levels the thousands of births
aren't noticed. Until one day, in one year, in one clutch

of eggs, under a rock in a single strip of desert, one male
lizard slides from the softened egg, feels a blinding sun

in its fresh eyes, raises and stretches its triangular head,
exposing an out-of-the ordinary orange throat, so unlike

its brothers that would soon struggle in vain attempts
to out-finesse him come the first mating season.

## The pair in the woods

traded some warm home clothing
for the nakedness of despair,
are night-bitten into clumps
of fresh battered flesh by daybreak,
day-bitten by angry flies
dispatched from the one true sun god
scolding anyone volunteering
for a month of such masochism.

The growing limb of nameless illness
turns a third eye on itself, wonders
on a newly borne face reflected in the green pond filth
disturbed by a rippling hand of thirst.

Hunger is that progressive skin and bones
installation at the new gallery we've heard about,
an archaic companion last witnessed
under the sure streetlights of safety,
where one steps from clean sidewalks
onto a film bus, is prepped up with a makeup
of dust and determination. Fright.

# The woods blindly fatten up

on bark song and limb whisper,
patient in wide waiting for falling sounds
to gentle down over hungry soil floor.

Animals help the night feeding,
clicking flattened teeth or fangs
with mouthfuls of soft river pebble,

claws tapping through softening clay,
paws sweeping fresh leaves away
so the ground might better follow

along, the music sometimes tending
a mind of its own before finally landing,
catching hovering eddies in the air,

fattening itself on the sight of sun
dappled woods and sightless trees
with endless mouths open at the roots.

## What did I want?

I can't remember asking myself this along the way.
The landscapes ruined by my thoughts, words, and deeds
long ago aren't named Lazarus.
                                        They've gone to rot.
No good buddy came around after I'd committed
my acts of immature betrayal, weeping for my shortcomings,
calling the body of my sins forth from the stinking tomb.

And what would I have wanted anyway, not knowing
any better one pain from another,
carrying the center of my world near my underdeveloped brain
and hyper-aware desires? My apparent reason for existing
being to avoid hurting by hurting,
                                        a young, stupid male animal,
loosed into a world of raw, hanging meat.

What did I want? Other than to hunt and consume?
To chew things up. To leave a trail proving my existence.

# Where were they going?

We might have been headed downtown,
when there were still plenty of reasons
for going to downtowns, or out to eat,

or leaving some busy parking lot, trying
to pull onto the highway dividing town
after a long day in Knoxville. I heard

father yell: W*ell, who let the gate open?*
A curious kid, I strained forward to see
what all the commotion was about,

wondering, hoping, some livestock
might be stampeding down the road
at us, but try as I might I only saw

the backup of traffic down the line
and the body language of impatience
behind the wheel as my father

attempted to merge with the flock,
and spotting no animals, I lost interest,
but not so much as to forget to inquire

where said gate was located and who
might be in charge of it and how long
so many cars full of families like ours

had been kept waiting up the road.
No one answered my "silly question."
No one *ever* explained mysteries to me.

# Backward Spiritual

Ella Gene lowers from the city bus
in her beat-up wheelchair, slight frame
wrapped thick against the mid-day winter wind,
head uncovered, shakes her skeletal hand
at the driver, knuckles visible a block away,
her *God bless, ye, honey,* whispered
through always ashen lips.
                            Takes to rolling,
edging backward, little-step-by-little-step,
across the parking lot, across the afternoon,
across mid-week, back and back her only means
of movement. Arms too weak, long ago.
Legs too week to pull her forward, long ago.
Having made the trip into town from the bus station
so many times, hardly having to look back.

Always sings out:
>                *Get that devil behind me, Lord!*
>                *Get that devil behind.*
>                *I can see him catching up,*
>                *my Lordy, runnin out of time.*

I yell out sometimes, Hey there, Ella Gene!
Poke that bastard in the eye that's chasing you!

She laughs on, sings out even harder,
usually forgets who I am by evening time

as she's making her way back to the station, singing, singing. Still not caught.

# The Orange-Throated Whiptail Considers

Was it a surprise, when the first tail popped off?
Was the lizard in chased, hiding, minding its business when half
its body length simply fell off and kept twitching.
Did both prey and predator stare in surprise at the new trick?
Did the halved animal sense some remaining connection
with the tail, a remote control, a residual phantom pain?
Was this an evolutionary event, this first instance, signaling
a forever change, not setting well with the animal, rebelling
at the DNA level in a manner so that every new tail-less animal
that was supposed to result was negated down the line?
Or was the loss of the tail fully planned by the first animal,
who hated its tail anyway, who found it got in the way
of getting away, who thought it too long or skinny or wide,
who was glad to realize it was loosening for whatever reason
and rejoiced when, turning a rock corner on a hot day,
came face-to-face with a saber tooth cat and, whipping
its tail so hard in panic, finished the job and scurried away,
only to feel it growing back by the next dangerous morning.

# Friday Night

We drive in the dark. Her hand flinches out
latching to my forearm,
                      expressing, *slow down*.

I notice colorized flashing through a bay window,
through sheerness thinner than the hint of a silk slip.

*Slower*, the hand urges.
                      A television looking
as big as the wall floods the house with its beats
of programming mystery, morphs dancing beings
between the screen's pop, the dark night air,
and her unashamed gaze.
                      *Slower*.

My brakes squeal a light hint at straining
alongside a row of mailboxes.

The silhouette of a woman crosses the stream,
interrupts our voyeuristic connection, leans
to the window and peeks out at the car
picking up speed down the neighborhood street.

# The cat's paw prints in this morning's snow offers no sound

The squirrel, two blocks away in its leaf ball nest, stirs
        in a dream of sunlight
The transient man with the heavy backpack just stepping off
        the bus onto the sidewalks of a new town, steadies
        himself on early day ice
The gentle persuasion of wind on snowfall, a raised eyebrow
The empty belly full of wonder about the next hour
The bass thump of a radio tune sensed across town feels like
        the hiccup of a strong heartbeat in the chest
The stacks of library books through the building's windows
        feel strangely like friends on the other side of a wall
The conversations behind eyes you know are there all day,
        seeking

# An Endurance III

For the sake of Saint George who slays the long red dragon
    of constant brake lights every night, we endure,

For the sake of that worrisome *tick, tick, snap* we've tried twice
    to act out to the mechanic to no avail, we endure,

For the sake of finding the source of the increasingly rank funk
    coming from under the passenger seat, we endure,

For the sake of weaving across six lanes in a quarter mile
    to make your exit or you're fucked, we endure,

For the sake of not staring too hard at your own reflection
    in the black shine of the motorcyclist's helmet visor,
    avoiding another close call with an existential moment
    when you should be concentrating on driving
    at five-thirty on a Friday afternoon, we endure,

For the sake of those whose commute makes them feel as if
    they live in the metal womb of their car, we endure,

For the sake of all those who actually live in cars, we endure,

For the sake of all those who will die in cars, we endure,

For the sake of all those who can't afford a car, we endure,

For the sake of those run over by cars while screaming
    for change, we endure,

For the sake of all hitchhikers, we endure,

For the sake of all animals, small and large, who try to pick
    the perfect instant to cross the busy road, and make it,
    or fail, or simply vanish as our headlights veer away,
    we endure.

# Daily Rhapsody

*After Barbara Ras's "Rhapsody Today"*

Maybe today a lightning strike in the midst of a snow storm
will startle you awake and once you're up moving around
you remember it's early May. Maybe today the groundhog
you watched in the backyard all last spring will return, but
for only a week. That will be enough of a hello, and it will seem
strange for a groundhog to be out and about playing
in snow, but the image will follow into this time next year
if you let it, just as you remember pulling over last year
into the city cemetery to photograph the first crocuses.
Maybe you'll not mind the cold, how the desire to pull
off your wool socks and walk into the yard feels like
something wonderful and unavoidable is about to happen
and that if you don't relent to the image of it, you'll cause
all the snow to melt prematurely. And maybe today you'll hear
the crows out back like usual, but pick up something new in
their croaks and trills, something familiar beyond
a nostalgia for a past life, but a translation taking place
in real time, as if you've woken up filled with some other
languages, but have to keep it to yourself or else the crows will
fly off forever. Maybe you'll finally find that lost ring
your grandmother gave your mother who gave it to you,
a ring they both wore until they were married, which is why you
have it now. Why not stop waiting today for a knock

at the door, an arrival of answers, a package emptied
of guesses, a fine disturbance in an otherwise uneventful living
out of questions.

# Some days it's that delicious parade

of mysterious misfits rivering up and down
the sidewalks, arguing politics into the air
with alcohol-sweet Holy Spirit tongues
on their bittered breath, bags of found wares
slung over backs looking like desperate tinkers
on the hustle. Other days it's not so romantic,
not so poetic and the floats lose their bearings
and stall down dead end alleys, the prize-winning
hometown bands show up confused, in tears,
too late and without scores. The homeless
grizzled man, fresh off the bus from out of town,
barely making it along on diabetic-endangered feet,
breaks down in sobs, hungry, hunching over
on the curb too closely to speeding traffic
and without the benefit of low background music.
Just wants to make it up another two blocks
to where he's heard there's a chance he can find
a HUD apartment. A woman reeking of cat piss-
like meth fumes enters the store with no drum roll,
eyes lolling, voice stuttering like a run out record
how she needs to sell the pretty metal box
she's tossed on the counter, swearing it's pure silver.
You know it's not. You sold it to her yourself
just last week for a dollar. You offer to buy it back
for seventy-five cents, which pisses her off.
As she calls you a damned son-of-a-bitch
she sobers for an instant and remembers

where she is, giggles and turns back to the door.
Returns to her warm and waiting spot in the parade.

# Dead cat circled in turkeys

We are the turkeys
pacing in a circle around the dead cat.
Still. No one told you this,
did they? With the craze of sensation
we generated on Youtube,
*National Geographic*, and *NPR*,
*The Mirror* and *The Sun*,
it seems they've neglected to inform you
of our tragic circumstance.
We're still out here. All day in the heat.
Nights in the dark. In our dizzying,
confining and confounding flock.
Journalists possess little
appreciation for what it's like
to keep one eye on the tail feathers
to one's front and the other eye
squarely on a creature
that was terrifying the neighborhood
that early morning in question.
We wonder, still, if it only sleeps.
We wonder, still, if it's the spell we now weave
keeping the beast mostly flattened to the road.
We wonder, still, if that lift of hair
along the swelling belly
was a sudden shallow new breath.
But no one will answer our questions
but us. And we are a confused lot. Not the man

who filmed us and started this unwanted fame,
not the news men and women still driving by
acting as if they don't see us. Still.

## There are no mile markers in space.

Nothing is sufficiently still.
No matter how thrust is perfectly timed,

the gentleness of robotic release,
all is flung from the original Great Center,

dark matter carrying all things invisibly.

All in sleep. All in waking. Entire
galaxies drifting intact, the same

gravity biding what keeps the atoms
of your clenched hand convinced

it's a hand in your traveling sleep,
your eye an eye during those long blinks.

Cast out something from yourself:
A quiet opinion, a glance, a muttering,

some sacrifice to the vacuum,
see how it races to keep up with you,

mirrors your trajectory, like a pet echo.

So calm yourself. You'll know
you're there when you get there.

# The Gods of Firsts and Companions

Summer's give is that last draw of aggravating sweat
    teasing the spine,
      ebbing dance with gravity, collecting

along each exploratory inch, soaking salt
                into the recent tightening
of a beltline. The final swatting away of unidentified
      swarms of irritation around ears and eyes,
            the old taste of gnats.

Be gone with the lot of this, we demand.
        Bring on the shift.
        Invite the season's best
final assault
        and end it.
        Just end it, please.

Do you know the moment close to September's
fluid meridian when the day turns
on an instant (is it a flip of a switch, or more
a gradual thing suddenly realized?)
                    I've noted this.

That first Autumnal shift, sneaking whisper

    behind my back, a giggle
    of playful arrival
    brushing skin,
    pleasant invading

into the nose, fast translated
into distractions.
                  Familiar. Yes.

    (Stowaway beings with messages,
    maybe. Is that it? Are they dancing
    along, minding their own time, then
    are swept up through the void
    into our space by a simple god nod?
    Given the job of notifying each
    of us one at a time if we've prayed
    hard enough and are paying attention.)


As much a scent as a feeling,
it remains outwardly unceremonious,
              but in my mind a quiet celebration

when I catch that fleeting reminder, wishing
to welcome it
in some improved manner every year,

    promising to mention it on a calendar,
    compare this day with the next year's
similar moment,

curious if it falls near a familiar date,
to establish that recognizing harmony with change.

                Curious if
an exactness exists at all, and in that, epiphany:

        The first crocuses, bumblebees,
        growth to full greening in the mountainside,
        the chicory swaying as trucks fly
        by on the highways,

a first cicada in the trees screaming its beg for company.

But I've yet to do this, this marking of time and date.

Never been sustained in the poetry of that flash
long enough to remember.
                            It fleets.

        (I've seen that glancing look in other eyes.
        That something just happened in the air, shared,
        but mostly missed, again. Then it's back
        to head's down, making way along sidewalks,
        the gods loitering on corners or passing in cars
        blinking and shaking their heads wondering,
        as they always do, what it's going to take.)

I've been dependably awful with dates
and names, holidays. I cannot tell you
the official arrival of Autumn.

>                          But I do know when
>                                I arrive at it.

I greet it in the wind.
Summer creeps up differently,
>               storing its humidity

to pounce one day while you're indoors, waiting
for you to come out.

>        (You should know when you're being
>        stared down. It's one of the first lessons
>        learned as a child. When you're taken
>        out and left on your own in the woods.
>        Remember? No, you wouldn't.
>        It's terrifying. Why would we want
>        to keep such memories? These
>        first fears, of a season, of a dying.)

Autumn is abrupt, a cool wind moving across,
>    decay's obvious and delicious hint. It digs
>    through your clothes, reaching for you,
>    taking a sample for a later reminder.

A hurricane brought Autumn in one year.
As the monster storm rolled and lashed
>                        closer to the east coast,

I tasted the lifted salt in the wind.

> (It is said: The gods sing in tastes.
> You might taste anything on the wind,
> salt, pollen, honey, blood, death.)

I swallowed it down to keep.

I can't let go.

# Menagerie

I'm fascinated by the odd abilities of animals.
Such as how fowl keep their heads in perfect
immobile position as their bodies move, like
the chicken jutting neck and head, thrusting
and halting, the body catching up, or better,
how a hummingbird's head locks into place
as it hovers and searches out a sweet drink.

Or the required patience of a crow attacked
in the air by the angry grackle. The unique
waddled scurry of low crawling creatures,
the alligator and lizard. The surprising speed
of bears. The intelligence in the eyes of horses
and whales. A snow monkey's meditative
hot springs practice. The tiny mayfly's full
life lived in only a twenty four hour cycle.

Might they wonder on any oddity of ours?
Our burial customs, worship of fire, grasping
of hands with laughter, our planned piercing
of one another's backs with sharp metals,
our staring into brightly lit boxes into the night,
our waving of bright flags in terrible times,
or our sworn denials of other's better futures.

# I turn on the early morning news,

watch the procession of the day's blood
begin, spilled overnight, sometimes
falling during broadcasts, still
warm on hands, on sidewalks, faces.

I keep a folded newspaper from yesterday
under my arm all day, like a spell,
or weapon against today's expected flow
of tear-fresh news, praying my rhetorical

questions: Wasn't yesterday enough?
And if not, can today suffice? Please?

We are brimmed with the unfathomable,
our young lined up neat and tidy
to the hilltop altar. Our young dropped

from planes into lands with strange names
where they die side-by-side. Our young
are numb and pulseless in the alleys
of great cities. Blood, simple blood,
knows no twenty-four hour news cycle.

It only knows our sheltered inner-space.
Or when it escapes to become spirit.

# Mid-Day Film Editing

A jet floods out a thin contrail beyond the foreground
of new tries of limbs shot up and wide
by last year's topped black locust tree.

I'm torn between taking it all in as: jet, trail, and tree.
Distracted man standing in driveway.

Or, letting a story stream in: of bamboo chimes,
squirrel play, and slow alley traffic:

as a truer soundtrack, but fearing
there is only a slight delay of the jet's rolling rumble
to come, or not

(who knows what will end up on the editing floor?),

I look to the promise of the apartment
front door only a quick three steps away.

# Re-Coil

Like a snake coiled and backing
into its self-assumption, you can attempt
to re-spring the mechanisms of regret,
confess and live harder, play harder, know
a thing clearer, like unmistakable heat-seeking.

Every few poems forward
set you reversed a hair, another devolution
of sorts, a very few work good
enough to see through to the scarred bone
and socket, to the skin-tightened contrivances
holding the epiphanies back.

So it's a back and forth thing you find,
mostly without thinking, as if
catching a trace of old helpful speech
as you fall back in trust, *there,*
                        *and there.*
Finding the moment fleeing.
                    *There, again.*

But to slow is to stop, which would break
the bones holding up the hunch you've held.

And the closer you get to the memory
of some things, the better the memory

of how a fear smelled. But you
left out too quickly
 with no rope. No map.

Bravely. Stubbornly. Coiled back convinced
you could re-live your mistakes, if
for no one else but you and that those
you wronged would somehow
forgive you
 magically through the fabric
of mystic universal love you think
waits on you hand and foot through
intentional thoughtfulness.

*Come closer,*
the universe says. *What do you see?*

# Today is Saturday. Pick your headline.

The next school shooting.
An exasperating early morning tweet
     by the president rattles stock market.
Director quits film after accusation.
A failed suicide / terrorist bombing.
The death of poetry.
Fake news.
*Onion* article quoted by a state legislator as truth.
You have a painfully ingrown toenail
     home remedies will no longer relieve.
NRA membership higher than ever, morally bankrupt.
AR-15 rifle debated as dangerous or not
     by fifth grade champion forensics team.
Contract signed amid rumors.
Accurate news.
Pay equality within reach by next year.
Man walks away from argument
     without losing sleep over it.
More Americans learning Chinese.
North Korean sends aid to US
     amid heightened tariff wars.
Oxford comma adopted as standard by Buddhism.
The next school shooting.

# I was warned in school against reading ahead:

> "Sorrow is knowledge: they who know the most
> Must mourn the deepest o'er the fatal truth,
> The Tree of Knowledge is not that of Life."
>
> Byron's *Manfred* (1817)

That it would spoil a story as surely
as a bar of chocolate might before supper,
like the sin of premarital sex. That it was cheating
to turn your exam paper over too quickly.

But I grew as fascinated with their obsessions
with my spoilage as by those objects
of supposed temptation, pursuing each
like a fleeting delicacy. I was grounded
after gorging on desserts, abandoning
untouched entrées. I forged ahead in reading,
by only a few lines at first, by paragraphs,
then by whole chapters. I couldn't help myself,
devouring *The Revelation* before *Genesis*
when we were assigned in Sunday School
the great task of reading the entire Bible.

My library card was taken when I was caught
detailing the ends of books to classmates
who needed help with their homework.
I was thrown out finally when they found me
in the aisles reading only the last pages
of each book. I wasn't hurting a soul,
but it creeped them out, seeing someone
peeping, getting ahead for once, seeing
what ought not be seen.
                                    I was reaching
for a kind of knowing, convinced that if only
I could see another page ahead, anticipate
some right thing, I'd figure out the big secret.
I'd know what they were hiding.

I'd know better why claiming this corner
every morning feels so right,
shouting out what the inner prophet sees:

don't turn down that block, not there, not yet,
or don't run that yellow light, not now,
after all this time, and, don't slurp that last sip
of coffee so quickly while opening the bank door
so slowly while distracted by that man's sharp suit,
young lady, after skipping so happily off
the city bus red line you should have missed.

If only I could have gotten to you in time.

# Let Off To Run, Part I

What animal strains to break the leash?

Under years-toughened earthen skin,
thickened with its own feud, a-feared
of unstopping its own smoke-confused nostrils.
Self-frightening, gnawing the truth
down into morseling marrows.

Try keeping it or relenting to its night
begging, free its neck bindings, set it off,

hear it tear hell over the howling ridge.

But things we track blindly down the black
tunneled brambles will kill us all off
if they corner us rightly, locked up in a fight

we won't let limbs free of, buried on the spot
under hard earned torn flesh whether ours or its.

Impossible to tell in there. Most blood smells

the same at first. You have to give it a few days.

# Micro-Biology

What rides on the slow bucking backs
of our cells? I know there's a being

hidden in Creation, yet mythologized,
deserving, patiently waiting, even yearning

if it has the capacity, craving the stardom
of inclusion on a list of discoveries.

And if there exists but one, there's another,
the several, then a legion as unfathomable

as heaven's blessed burgeoning host,
every winged shoulder, strained back

and thigh, reminded by the pain of lifting
glory ever high enough as to be invisible

as a single cell fighting off its wild rider.

# I sip my Red Stripe beer, as usual,

always on a Monday or Thursday, the jukebox to my back,
the crowd loud to my left, my head down as I'm drawing

little cartoons on my phone, animals, caricatures of drinkers
down the bar. They leave the door open on days like this

to let out the heat, though it's in the forties. Three quiet TVs
color the room with jerky sports movement. The Olympics

are on. Women's hockey. The woman to my left plays cards
her phone, leaves her son a message. She usually leaves me

to drink in peace, unless I'm in the mood to talk. I joke once
about the day's politics. She doesn't get my humor. We grow

quiet, she leaves, I return to my drink, sketching Trump out
like a clown. A fellow poet drops in and the night is saved.

# The Changing

*For Jessica*

Do you write      between kicks, or
use tiny knocks as accents      on syllables?
The rests as long vowels, this newly alive alliteration.
Do you sort of feel as if you're writing
to yourself, mirrored, when musing
on that first ultrasound,     like an outline
of words?
             Do you read out loud now,    speak
to the being curling, stretching within,
through the shared, membrane:
mutual hearing and teaching and learning?

What transpires through that thin line of poetry,
within the quieted, muffled word:

      a first and newer language?

When did you realize
    you can never just talk to yourself?

# Along Middle-August, Summer Thinks

some on fading, you may walk incidentally through
invisible clouds of seasonal time, sweet-scented
like suspended rot, a small floating spot caught

under a shading oak or willow, where smears
of light over only a few hours a day roll by,
but not too much, just long enough to boil a bit

the vining and webbing of roots in the shallow puddles
seemingly never drying up, the source of that perfume
you catch, like a reminder of primordial otherness,

a soft taste swept into your mouth with the wind,
kept there for the rest of the day, into rest. Into sleep.

# They Call Me

I am called The Clutch. I am
kept cool in the ancient box
fashioned of plywood and screen,
hinged as simply and purposefully
as my perfect fanged jaw, created
by and of the loving Hand of God.
I will do as I will when provoked,
when the air is perfumed
with sweat and song, with notes
of fear and longing on fire
in summer nights, electrified.
I am hungry for your pain.
I melt the flesh from your trembling hand.
I was born unknowing death, held
in my mother's mouth, the light
of The Lord's poison dripping
from her thinly columned hate.
Call me from my sleeping box.
Rattle me over your head, in the sky,
under the noses of the god you tempt.

# Familiarity

It rains here around this time
every evening.

The day,
like a tired woman,

winds down,
slows,
chills from a vibration
dropping in the air,

familiar, like
yesterday,

notices blackened sky
rolling up, over
through flipping leaves.

Watches browned leaves
of the day fall
twisting in the kicking wind.

The first splats
of rain come as a jolting
sip of ice water
can be,

surprising, though we drink
every day.
        And forget.

# I Divine

I can tell what you'll have for lunch tomorrow
    by tasting the leftover salt on an eyelash
    you plucked from your lid after you fought
    over a jealous something-something
    he's already forgotten and you've forgiven.

I know your middle name by the way you avoid
    answering public pay phones, though most
    people do now, but you won't because
    of a secret you're still keeping.

I had a dream last night about one of your best friends
    and how you'd had a dream about one of your
    best friends having a dream about one of their
    best friend's dreams being about losing touch
    with best friends.

I can estimate how long a body's been in the ground.
    Trust me on this one.

I am the seventh son of a seventh son and I never knew
    my father. Because of this I am supposedly gifted
    with something, but if I tell anyone what it is,
    I'll lose that special power. FML.

I learned to water witch from my great aunt Velma.
    She died of heatstroke, lost in the Mojave Desert

after her car broke down. Her husband,
my great uncle Jimmy, a retired mechanic,
had stayed home, giving her some time on her own.

# Swamp at Cape Fear

Where the angry waves of salt mostly halts
at the island forest, against stubborn dunes
concerted with tall pines and live oak, some

of the sea is fooled in to the reedy swamp,
trapped since the last storms, edges blended
with a fresh lake. Here is a mingling home

for the old words: brackish and frothing,
an incessant death, corruption of the flesh,
a struggle for rooting in a lacking light,

wheezes and huffs of black water logged
heavy animals and the eyeful hungered
slinking of near invisible things in weeds.

Here the tail whip just below the surface.
Here the unblinking eyes watching just
above the algae scutted surface barely

mirroring the cloudlessness of sky above
in its odd unspotted blue. There the rusty
hue of a thing dead in blend with a thing

living, a feeding and feeding. What of all
this boiling in the elemental soup? What
can possibly be born from its pulsing mud

in the warm womb of waiting muck, up
bubbling there, and there, stenching filth
alive with the sacred assurance of soaked

sedimentary creation, leveled on itself each
season, taking what dares swim too deep
to escape the olden words it dredges awake.

# A teaspoon of the star's collapsed core weighs a billion tons

What lives on the foamy crested waves of silence between words, sensed, but muted by a dark coast without as much as a star's blink from a lighthouse, void of a single flash? Can a portion of heart, light in gladness or panged heavy of guilt carry a weight, even if unspoken, the mass roiling on like a mind's maelstrom, circling, quickening, finally self-aware, birthing its own centered gravity, collapsing one day upon itself, solidifying heavier metals, chunks, memories sinking, searching and finding one another, planeting over and over, failing and failing, colliding, rearranging in blindness: a question answered in time.

# Railroad Song

To pay mindfulness newly: every hair
living along your arms, riding your head,

dancing up, clothing incapable of preventing
the world from finding way to your lately

attentive, listening skin: mountainous
under-rumble, ear-swell, a squeaking,

sudden release; vast hissing to diesel hum,
this chest hugging surprise, *chink, chink,*

*tap, tap,* tapping; and the fumes, *Oh,
God,* the fumes, hated, remembered;

there, *Clank – jolt.* Hollow bounce to more
clanking, more rhythmic, metaled

determination, always dependable.
Demanding a quieting of all it passes.

Rumble to thunder. Dogs barking, crows
silenced. Bassy empty cars, scraping to spark,

out-birthed from this hill's heart-lined tunnel
of lightless questions: vibrations; ripping

through the ground to find the soles of feet;
to toe-tickle.  Light of day bone-quaking, growl.

Chain rattle and *thump, thump, ting.* Clock
work pendulum, grinding to a pitch, shaking

stones and dirt earth; gravity aching down
the heavy shaken tracks; vanishing red flash,

wheels on steel dying off, miles away
to whispered horn bursts we question

were ever really by here an instant ago.

# Murakami Steak & Eggs

"Rocket Man" plays on the restored Wurlitzer jukebox in the corner of the Waffle Town Restaurant. Hoshi can make out the sizzling of his ordered steak and eggs through the room's mixed chorus tune, behind conversation down the bar. The waitress, Sally, sasses the short order cook about speeding it up. The cook used to run the now defunct urban men's wear shop in the mall. That's where Hoshi knows him from. He's got on a tight knock-off brand shirt, two-days grease-stained and a crusty work apron. Bleached hair. Yep, that's Randle. It's obvious he's sweet on Sally. But so is Hoshi. Every time Hoshi leaves his dependable ten dollar tip, even if it's only black coffee with sugar he's ordered, it's his way of expressing admiration for Sally. Randle and Sally both mouth Elton John while the tornado warning plays on the muted evening news up on the wall-mounted TV. Hoshi will teach his history class this evening at the local community college. He's not fully prepared, but it's a subject he's taught what seems a hundred times – The Cold War Space Race. The wind kicks up outside. He watches the signal lights swing above the passing cars in the intersections, the sun setting quickly behind it all. Thinks he should get his steak and eggs to go so he can get to school earlier, be prepared better. A steel trashcan tips and rolls with a series of bangs before slamming into someone's car out in the parking lot. Everyone inside, startled with a jolt, turns and strains to see out the front windows.

# The Rumor

The sun is mostly set and it's still ninety degrees,
a day that's humid and thick, enough to really agitate
the virility out of the male cicadas. You're driving

with the windows down to smell the realness of air
and hear the animal chorus over the traffic, the change
in their way, in twos and threes, with each turn

of a block. With a curve westward, just so up a hill
where the view unpeels, you see the sunset explode
of scarlet and peach, blue bolts jetting from hills,

and wonder if all the pitch and hum thrumming out
of the mountainsides maybe aren't insects at all,
but more of an event of synesthesia you've only

heard of in poetry all your life but never believed.

# Let Off To Run, Part II

Turn on it, in the middle of the trail. Let it know
you've quit running somehow. Catch its dirty
chasing scent and stalk it backwards on the path.

Catch your breath. Squat and learn of it a while.
What this stalking thing is, is not proud death,
but a killing, choking thing, so mindless and slow
even the kudzu outruns it in time. But we tire

and succumb to sleep and it never stops for rest
in its over-creeping way. When it finds you, you
have to fight it like you found it first. That's why

you can't chase it running. And when it digs in,
you must unearth yourself calmly, or risk startling
that otherness away before tasting first blood.

# We Learn from History

I'm helping my father move boxes
from the house to the truck at the curb.
I point out a dead bird I've been stepping over.

Birds have been falling dead at this spot
under this powerline intersection for years, he says,
recalling how the man once owning the place
would point out the dead birds to him years ago.

Then I remember seeing them myself,
right here, as a kid, under this crossing
of lines, fascinated with the random mystery
of death just appearing on the ground.

There must be a break in the line up there,
he figures. For forty damn years? I wonder.
You'd think the birds around here
might have invented the song word
for danger after so many generations.

# Night & Day

> "The night has a thousand eyes,
> And the day but one"
> Francis W. Bourdillon

Drag the night in like slow wool, drag
the night out like a hungry dog, drag

the day by the hair of the head, angry,
out of the house, trick it fully, prankish,

trick it partly enough to get a foot out
and caught in the slamming door. Drag

the night back in after its worn out, tired,
eaten its fill of daylight and is homesick.

# I've been grounding myself lately.

*Earthing*, as some call it. The theory:
that we've insulated our battery bodies
too well from the planet's natural charge,
disconnected after all the progress made
with protective synthetic plastics,
rubberizations, and animal hide-soled shoes
for our precious little feet. In essence,

starving our once better electrified bodies
from the river of electrons whispered
from the soil, as if some entity,
like our own negatively charged doppelganger
still exists just under the crust we tread,
waiting patiently, invisibly, to root up
and bathe our toes and heals with voice

and planet reasoning. No wonder
children lose their shoes all the time
playing in the fields. No wonder we find
the strange among us shoeless on the roadside,
yelling at traffic in tongues we hardly remember.

## Yellow Found

I walked over the entire three acres of cemetery land,
the middle of the city, like back when graveyards began
in the center of towns, this one well over a century ago,
town founders near the middle with over-watcher obelisks
and squares and compasses and bold old names, lichens
patching along the corners of chipped but well-made
stones purchased with old money still around in town,

but I could not find another tiny patch of yellow crocuses
like I'd found at the entrance on that mid-February day
no matter how I searched, these fooled out of the ground,
tempted out, like the beams of sun this day and the warmth
finally on my face as I moved out from under the cedars.

# I like waking up early

when the idea of a true darkness
is almost believable and before
the coming blue light finds me

tries me shadowed in duplication
it's a soft seeking at first
through the vertical lack of light

up the hill where the birds
go about their first noisy stirs

it goes cottony white before long
trying my form at the desk
near satisfied it's found me again

just as it tried yesterday morning
hopefully tomorrow again

but the voice remains feeble
for a time still latched to night
growing that hand of heat

gripping over the hill finally
finding itself as we all must do
burning off my softer edges
all the easier to slice into shadow
find our names again in the sun

# Youtube: The Hand of God

To label it an *All-Seeing Eye* would be too obvious.
Looking on is too passive an act, even for gods.
No, the All Mighty uses this roving tool to hunt
down all the resultant extremes of an All Powerful fit
of creating still echoing through the hearts of human beings.
Through hearts into minds and hands and legs, out
of mouths with brilliant ideas: *Here, hold my beer.*

We are that mass civilization of famous failures
failing, on purpose, accidentally, all the in-between,
the All Father watching curiously from a window,
refusing to intervene: *They need to learn for themselves, honey.*
But, too, never abandoning the greatest-of-the-greats.

God so loves the world, that he scribbles
in that language only a god would understand,
the list of potential specimina to choose from
when all the best and worst of us are raptured up
to crowd the endless lands behind Heaven's gates,

examples videoed since the dawn of back yard wrestling
and snapped bones at the bottom of nearly won
trick steps by the No Skating signs. *Go ahead,*
God probably giggled to himself all day long.
*They didn't really mean it. It's worth your fifteen minutes
if you survive.* And if you don't, he's got a cage
waiting for the best of you along the "Avenue of Extremes."

The heavenly host sing infinite praises, shouting, *Ooh! Ahh! Ouch! Doh!*

*Pay me now, pay me later, but we've got an appointment to settle. Keep up the good work, everybody.*

# Creekside

Learning what should be called a creek. Or a stream.
Or river. Let's say it has to do with how far
a boy can cast a lure across water and get tangled up.
Yank at it, but end up cutting bait. Let the current
take the line floating downstream out of the way, slow
to the bottom rock and grasses. A boy's time
can run short with too much of this, the thing spooling out.
Let's call it a little growing up each summer.

# Being

I want to do
what scares me to death.

Like the little gray moth does each morning.
Trusting, nearly blind to the world.

Mottled in a hue of blue steel,
almost too small to be seen,
it could just as easily be a butterfly for all I know,
glancing its color is like looking
to the rain-promised darkening sky,

flitting and then lost
down in an overnight suddenness
of carpeting violets.

The gust of wind comes, uninvited,
over the back of your hand,
your neck, indeed,
                mundane,

but deadly enough to a tiny thing
pulled up and joining what we'd only know
as a gentled breeze,

we lumbering giants
making way through the long wood,

yet we've seen a smallish portion of this struggle
and it, too, now deserves story.

I want to go to the woods
and stretch my arms
around the largest tree I can find,

small like that being,

in the middle of a snow storm, waking
it with the crisping press
of my ear's flesh to the freezing bark. To stay

until I hear a new thawing
within this realm I try inhabiting,

that inhabits me, until my own voice alters,
speaks back. Frightens me to an attention.

Orders me out, to leave.
Orders me to live.
To go back

and do what scares me to death. Over and over.

# Reading a New Poem

Can you barricade in your breath
and fall back into shuttered eyes,

past where the visions surface
into view? Go in willingly, out

of your own senses, down the alley
to some stacks and piles of junk

gathered together only for you.
Strip open the sacks of discarded

living, their scents, sounds. Bathe in it.
Pull on an old coat, boots. Some hat.

Allow the slow abduction. Invite it
all in for sweet enjambment's release,

for the pretty, gentle conceit of it all,
realize then you're barely holding on.

# The Morning's Crow Math

A faint metallic echo
from the neighbor's property:

I turn as the crow's partner
squawks in surprise, pain,

the pellet-struck-crow crying out
as it falls from where it enjoyed

a high morning view. It was like
those black and white films recreating

First World War aerial dogfights,
the production model bi-planes

so light they plummet and spin
in the oddest ways,

as gravity eventually pulls them
to the ground, looking as if

the landing never ends
in flames and death.

# Birth Right

The grass fights underground,
back from sleeping brown root,

under-space, dry drought world,
land-flipped mirror time, loosed

by fresh warmth, bluing, now,
knowing, newly, green dreams

waiting out, up there, spiny veins
of tiniest reaches up to the blue,

upwards, a blue asking above,
just short of green, blue shading,

cooling blue, tree speaking blue,
where grains jump from the tips

of grass, to the juice of blue light.

# First Come, First Served

Evolution might
only be a lottery drawing
at the local gene pool,
a blind drawing
from the well-shaken Bingo tumbler:

B3 – a straight, spiraled horn,

G6 - the only insect with 3-D vision

the spare grassland watering hole,
those lucky of the herd
thirsty enough to make it
to the muddy bank
and not get pulled in by a Nile croc:

I5 – Most pounds per square inch in a bite

B1 - a hinged, spring-loaded
sticky tongue as long as one's body.

The one spotted hyena left behind
genetically predisposed
for urban domestication.

The first polar bear gone fully white:

C3 – poison blood,

B2 – Bi-pedal,

C5 – a taste for murder.

# Interpretation

Muddy death river
call us all in to dream,
wade along shadow pools
under a tree root dance

Careful with toes,
follow the beaver sound,
surprised slap of the tail,
the falling branch
or serpent upon the mud

Feed the water with fish,
swim and swim
back to birthright, breathe
in a clearer flowing

Find a shore line
familiar with family,
white-robed with hums,
hands high, hearts held

Carrying river stone,
chapel doors flung open on the hill,
sky written in stained glass,
clang of the single bell

Cemetery gate rusted,
always open
fresh earth, clay,
waiting for us

A scent of new cut flowers
in still air, a weeping,
a joyful noise

Shovels resting

# Between Worlds

Toward this effort of knowing, the dead
invoke our help from the shadow, and us
their service in turn: Here, nearer this gate

I am going, they say, where I may lose you
and more of myself, and I'll depend on you
to hold fast the meaning of my words,

though disembodied, the rich in flesh.
To travel along, interpret the journey,
requires holding fast the opposite corner
of the new veil, as partner, both of us steady,

peeking over at once hand-in-hand, frightened,
into what may be the surprise of wholeness,
traveling the grand thinness, the veil's tread-line

into the gated mystery, into the fog that lists
between all the words in the world about how
to live with the dead. And with the living.

## Azure Cold

Bowie plays for the fifth day in a row.
                                                           Can't say
I'd change the channel. I'm weeping like everyone does,
Surrounded with these panes of glass,
                                          a floating gallery,
A café craft
    (*can you hear me…*)

As town rushes by, the wind chill dipping dangerous,
        Suddenly, catching us all off guard, like
                Surprises                    love to do.

Tallest thing out in the azure starless day
Is a church spire reaching for all it's worth,
Its high cross marking a spot in the upward blankness,

Making me wonder what might be up there
                                        When the sun
                                              Sets,

What constellations might be pooling up
To pay homage in time, jetting some song our way,

Or if some spirited resonance is newly orchestrated,

                On its way by a new strumming hand.

# The Same Question, Again.

Isn't there supposed to be a single element, at least
some universal material, old as heat or dark or color,
falling down over it all, webbing across the histories

of wherever we step, wherever our fingers and bodies
and eyes touch, into every last lightless turn we make
and meander through the halls, incorporated into all

the tastes and all that must not be tasted, into thought,
out over all the untrodden fields like a foot-high fog
with no intention of going anywhere. And if it doesn't

dwell out in that *there*, wouldn't it want to eventually,
or have at some time past, remembering itself, how
essential the world requires invisibility holding fast?

# Bosch Studies on Monsters I, II, & III

Would we want to wonder too long
on what portion of a late-Middle Ages mind,
already long steeped in horrors, reaches

even deeper into the dark to find a hell
full of extra third and fourth legs
to attach to squatish rat and troll bodies,

ratchets stretched trunks to the faces
of whale bodies? Are we allowed
such curiosity, granted a secretive glance

through a side channel view of true Hell,
finding every demon burdened in glops
of still-damp oil tints, eternally drying,

visages never finished, no matter
how the damned heat boils: is this
where color has retreated? Where only

charcoal exists? How underworld bodies
forever try claiming themselves
when birthed as screaming sketches?

# Peck: A making of stars

*After Ted Hughes*

Crow was giant, holding the earth
in its bloating belly, full of itself
and the rumor of having to birth
some civilization from its own gut
or be alone for eternity in the black.

Crow strained as it grew, heavier
in words, heavier in deeds, in blood.
In confidence with a view of future.

Crow barked out on the only limb
it found, clawing at the hold,
stretching its neck out for no one,
for everyone that would be someone.
Calling on the swift spirits,
calling them down from stars.

Crow watched the dark, turning
black to black, as it wretched
in its own nothing, felt sudden
punches in its gut, knowing life
was nearly ready to try breath.

Crow knew the young ones would
crave light, as Crow once had,
stared up feeling eyes crossing
in the black, stabbed up its long beak,
punching holes in the nothing,
letting the mystery of light crash
through to feed a new soul
with every arrival, holding close
its breath, keeping the flow of water,
blood back, counting out names,
a hundred-billion, pecking out
a night sky for thriving under.

# The Baby Visits

My wife cradles our niece's newborn son
in her lap. It's hard to distinguish
whose *coos* are whose. Everyone is speaking
the gentle language of *goo* and *gaa*.

I've walked through on the way
to my study with a bad case of hiccups.
They erupt from me intrusively.
Loudly, painfully.
I am an obnoxious intruder.

My noise almost wakes Gabriel,
mostly asleep now, happy with a belly full
of warmth, body swaddled with a blanket,
curled safe in my wife's protection.

He makes noises all his own,
his own words of tiny grunts.
Then he's suddenly got the hiccups.

And mine have ceased. What must a tiny being
wonder when stricken with these mysterious jolts
of sound from the gut, waking one
from warm goodness? It will learn

cute *awws* and *owws* for sure
from his aunts and cousins, his mother,
but *ouch*, from the painful hiccups,
from his uncle, the loud, obnoxious one
who it contracted the mystery
from in the first place.

Let that be the story.

# These Things

The knock of bamboo chimes
as the creep of mortality.
Falling single leaves in summer lushness
when no one watches.
Burning poetry books
for heat in the night.
Pleading for help in a language
no one understands.
An undisturbed mound
under a carnival merry-go-round.
The pipe bomb
found on a walking trail.
An old hall lined with game mounts
with antlers still projecting hate.
Perfectly formed, positioned, and timed:
chunks of deadly hail.
Bills accumulating on the dresser
never opening themselves.
That first moment of memory loss
mistaken as *just tiredness*.
Unmistakable smoke of leaves in autumn
or a winter house fire.
The lost charging cord.
The dying phone.
Coffee grounds and cat dander.
Skin flakes and eye lashes.
Having to choose - then choose again.

Hair found on a pillow.
You promised they were all gone.

# What Slight Dissonance

The sun gives out,
preparing the dark
along flat desert sands,
for the green sliding of hills,
inside the leafless silhouettes
of wintered mountainsides.

We ride the sun down,
light flees, the dark bursts
that hidden dam and fills our eyes
and heads with songs of night
shadow hinting the same promise
as last evening, and before.

But it's how the night forms
turn in medley once the sun goes
missing that makes up
our personal worlds, our cultures:
movement in sunlessness,
our unique darkness, the story.

# Telling the Humans

Our folklore speaks of *Telling the Bees*
when someone passes for fear of their
up and abandoning the hive, seemingly
neglected in the funereal rites of the family,
left out of the grieving process, the sitting up
all night, the long flight to the waiting hill.

But who can we tell of bee death? This
mysterious so-called Colony Collapse?
What human being waits for word
that yet another hive fails out in the trees
or out in the field of the old couple's farm?
Should one receive word or many?

What ancient honey bee carries
the black shawl and the song?

And how would we know the morning had come
when such word was simply undeliverable.
That a certain music went missing in the night,
a certain shift in all things,

       sleep, step, earth.

# Eroding to Sleep

The body hints of flagging
on the drift, sleep is a threatened storm,
hinted of heat bursts over the black water
too far out to know for sure, with waves

tiding in sweeps to find floating things,
separate them into parts
on an eddy's private schedule,
an eventual wet salted
clunk and slosh of parted bone,

softened sinew, blanketed of thunder,
the working out of things making themselves known,
water warmth working up the marshes,
red-fingered blood deltas searching at something,

once inland needing back out of land,
the desire of washing up on beaches forgotten,
a life deep where they've been dredged a mile out,
forgotten, morphed to shoreline. A new body.

## Sunken Ground

You can take a lot to your grave. Secrets.
Unshared things. Selfish choices. Moments
unspoken. And that spot waiting for you
bloats with every whisper you insist on taking

with you, each conversation to work out
in your sleep-talking when you can't stretch
your legs anytime
    you want. When they'll
only let you up for pacing to think out
your problems after the bells sound darkness,

when the ground you vacate for a while
sinks behind you since you drag your riddles
with you, never discarding what you brought
to that spot once the lid closes on your choices.

Repeat: *Once the lid closes on your choices.*

So give it all up, I say. Claim a lighter casket
when the time comes. Let the ground sink
even when you're down there sleeping well.

## Let's agree

those screams
landing on us,
that we absorbed

when we were pulled
through the womb-gate,
were celebratory,

and let's agree
we forgot that pain
of sudden gravity
yanking us to the ground
after swimming
for so very long,
and the cold room,
the glares of stainless steel
tables and machines,
and strangers' hands,

abandoned the pain
like they say
mothers can
of birthing agony.

Let's agree
the discomforts
lived then

are too far buried
back in the mind
to have rooted
into your adult choices.

Let's agree
a first warmth,
that suckling hug
is what all the surprise,
the discomfort,
was really about,

and carry that memory,
if we can find it again,
into the hateful world.

# About the Author

Larry D. Thacker's poetry is in over 150 publications including *Spillway, Still: The Journal, Valparaiso Poetry Review, Poetry South, The Southern Poetry Anthology, The American Journal of Poetry, The Lake, Illuminations Literary Magazine,* and *Appalachian Heritage.* His books include three full poetry collections, *Drifting in Awe, Grave Robber Confessional,* and *Feasts of Evasion,* two chapbooks, *Voice Hunting* and *Memory Train,* as well as the folk history, *Mountain Mysteries: The Mystic Traditions of Appalachia.* His MFA in poetry and fiction is earned from West Virginia Wesleyan College. Visit his website at: www.larrydthacker.com

www.ingramcontent.com/pod-product-compliance
Lightning Source LLC
Chambersburg PA
CBHW022012120526
44592CB00034B/789